BUILD YOUR OWN
PIRATE SHIP

Model engineering by Pat Doyle
Colour artwork by Inkwell Studios
Other illustrations by David Woodroffe
Text by Karen Farrington and Nick Constable

THE FIRST PIRATES

PIRATES HAVE BEEN AROUND ALMOST SINCE man learned to sail. Thousands of years ago, the Egyptians and then the Greeks and Romans documented accounts of robbery at sea. Their ships were raided by bloodthirsty crews roaming the Mediterranean Sea, who even captured the great Julius Caesar himself. He was held prisoner until their ransom demand was met.

But the age of the pirates really took off in the 16th century when Spanish galleons, returning from the New World, laden with treasure, exotic spices or fine cloth, fell prey to the robber ships. Piracy was the most certain way for a sea captain to get rich quickly. The Spanish Main, North Atlantic, Mediterranean Sea and English Channel became desperate places for merchant ships trying to reach home ports.

The China Sea and the west and south coasts of Africa also became dangerous areas for shipping. The merchant ships were often well defended, and sometimes escorted by warships, but they were no match for a determined attack by a collection of pirate vessels working together.

The attackers would hoist the feared skull and crossbones flag, known as the Jolly Roger, which first appeared on West Indian waters around 1700. It was supposed to offer the target ship a chance to surrender, but if it refused, the pirates would haul up a crimson flag which meant: 'Get ready to die.'

Such tactics were designed to undermine the spirit of merchant sailors and frighten them into surrender. The skull and crossbones was a very common symbol on gravestones at the time and the mere sight of it was often enough to leave crews begging their Captain to give up.

Some famous pirates tried to spell out how ruthless they were by adding their own well-chosen designs to the flag signals. Blackbeard had a skeleton with an hourglass in its hand, to show that time was running out for his opponents. Others used cutlasses, daggers or hearts dripping with blood.

To make matters worse, the monarchs of the major seafaring nations didn't seem too bothered about stamping out the cut-throat business. *They* had a habit of employing their own pirates (known as privateers), who would pay a cut of their ill-gotten gains to the Crown. In those days corruption was rife and any Captain who did get caught by a naval patrol could often bribe his way to freedom.

When pirates arrived in a port there was little risk of them being reported to the authorities. Many towns and villages owed their prosperity to the pirate bands. Wealthy gentlemen would invest in a planned voyage of plunder, local traders would sell the wares brought back, while others would supply any gunpowder, food or fuel the pirates might have ordered.

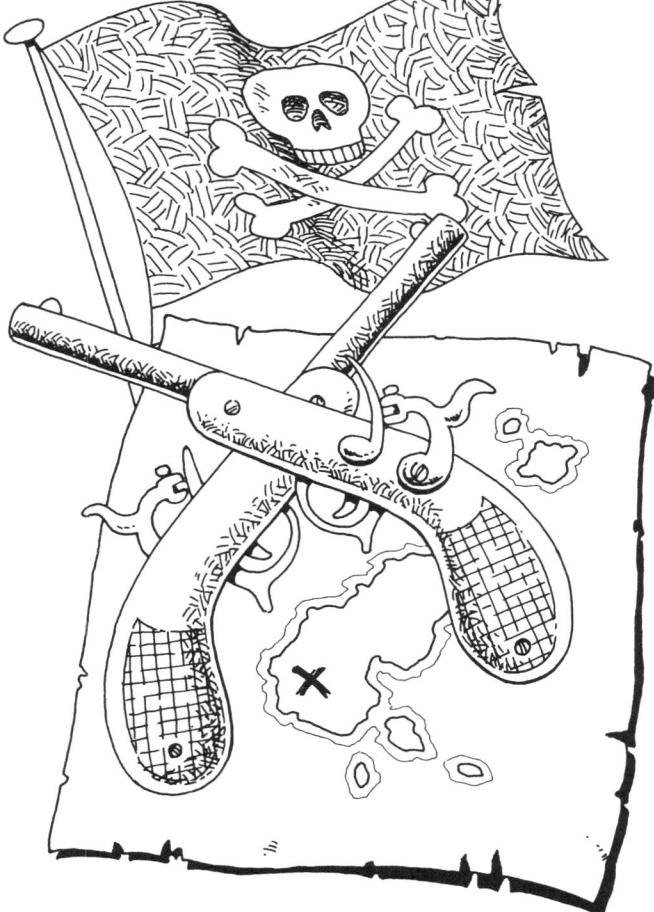

When the honest law enforcers tried to prosecute these pirates, they were greeted with silence and threats of more violence by those whose livelihood depended on these illegal activities. Juries would rarely convict an accused man for fear of revenge. Unsurprisingly, the number of pirates multiplied.

 # LIFE UNDER THE JOLLY ROGER

PIRATE CAPTAINS LIKED TO INCLUDE non-English speakers in their crews. A Frenchman, Dutchman, Turk or African was useful as a translator and sometimes they could find the most valuable cargo in a ship without even needing to utter a threat. Simply by listening to the talk of captured foreign officers – who would be unaware their conversations were being eavesdropped - the translator could tell his pirate shipmates details of the cargo hold. He might also pick up other information, such as the possibility of more merchant ships in the area.

The remainder of the crews would be ordinary young men who wanted to find a quick fortune. Apprentices would learn sea-craft aboard a small coaster and then perhaps progress to a privateer and finally a pirate vessel. Adventure on the high seas was also an attraction, with the added advantage that there was less of the ruthless discipline found on military ships. The strictest rule was that all men received an agreed share of booty. This form of honour among thieves was respected by most of the outlaw captains.

There were other hard and fast rules. This list is a summary of a 'code of conduct' drawn up by the men of Bartholomew 'Black Bart' Roberts, who roamed the Atlantic between the Caribbean and East Africa.

1. All major decisions should go to a vote.
2. Any thieves on board to be marooned as soon as possible. (This usually meant being abandoned on some lonely shore with only a gun, ammunition and water.)
3. All weapons to be kept scrupulously clean.
4. No women on the ship.
5. Anyone deserting his post in the midst of battle to be marooned or executed.
6. No fighting among the crew. All disputes to be settled on land.
7. Captain and Quartermaster to receive two shares of total booty, the Master Boatswain and Gunner one and a half shares, lower-ranking officers one and a quarter shares and all others one share apiece.
8. Compensation for injuries. (Loss of a limb would mean a £400 pay-off.)

Pirates adopted the same ranks and duties as seamen aboard naval ships. But there was one very important difference - they elected their Captain and could also sack him when they wished. His word was law only during battles.

OTHER RANKS ON BOARD A PIRATE SHIP

QUARTERMASTER: He was also elected by crewmen, and his duties included dividing up the booty and disciplining offenders. Though punishments were less common (and generally less brutal) than on naval vessels there were still some appalling practices. These included flogging with a whip called the 'cat-o'-nine tails', made from nine pieces of flayed rope. Still more severe was the 'tongue-o'-fire' in which a man's mouth would be stuffed with tar-soaked rope and set alight. Finally the Quartermaster could order a 'keel-hauling'. This involved tying rope round the victim, tipping him over one side of the ship and dragging him up the other. This meant the half-drowned man would be scraped against razor-sharp barnacles on the ship's hull. A very painful punishment.

LIEUTENANT: He served as deputy master of the vessel in battle and took charge in the event of the Captain's death.

BOATSWAIN: He was responsible for the smooth-running of the ship, including allocations of food and rum.

SAILING MASTER: His job was to keep the sails in good order, supervise men at work on the rigging and - most important of all - navigate.

CARPENTER: The vessel's odd-job man and one of his oddest jobs, assuming there was no ship's surgeon aboard, was to perform amputations on wounded crew. The only anaesthetic for this operation was rum ... and not even pirates' rum could kill the pain for the unfortunate patient.

GUNNER: He was in charge of hiring and training the gun crew - the men with the most dangerous job on the ship. Two- or three- tonne cannons would be lashed into position with rope, but every time they fired they recoiled, putting huge strain on their bindings. Sometimes a cannon broke free and rolled about below decks. Anyone who got in the way would be crushed and so the gun crew exchanged wills when they knew a battle was looming.

A pirate's life meant many other hardships. The disease scurvy, caused by a lack of fresh food, was rampant. Fish and meat were always revolting because they had to be so heavily salted in order to preserve them. Bread was never available because it went stale too quickly, so pirates were often reduced to a diet of ship's biscuits towards the end of a long voyage. These would become infested with insects over the months at sea and there were stories of pirates munching their dinner in the dark so that they wouldn't be put off if they saw a weevil boring its way out.

Rats were another nuisance. They thrived in the damp, stinking bilges and added to the problem of disease. It was said a Captain would always try to steal a merchant ship's medicine chest before its treasure chest because he knew it could keep him in business. Sometimes half a crew would die of diseases such as typhoid, scurvy, yellow fever and malaria.

Most pirates joined a ship by choice but occasionally one was pressed into service. This was particularly true of skilled shipwrights, whose services were much in demand. Such men would be lured aboard a ship with the promise of a voyage and the chance to work somewhere in the sun. In fact, as soon as the vessel left port, it would head by arrangement to a pirate den where the shipwright would be given little choice but to join the band and hope for the best.

Easy money; fancy dress

Successful crews often found themselves in a port with more money than they knew what to do with. They took to buying the most flamboyant and colourful clothes as a way of telling the world how rich and clever they were. They would strut about the docks wearing sword scabbards inlaid with the finest gold and jewels. Their shirts and cloaks would be of satin or silk, their breeches decorated with gold lace, their hats outrageous in style and jackets fastened with shining gold buttons. Many would show off fancy jewellery (perhaps this is why we imagine pirates wearing a gold ear-ring). It was hardly surprising that crowds would flock to the ports when a known pirate band had docked - just to catch sight of them and marvel at their wealth.

Savagery at sea

For all their finery, and the adventurous life they led, it must be remembered that most pirates were villains capable of appalling behaviour. In one act of savagery a vessel from Dort, in the Netherlands, was ambushed and boarded off the east coast of England. The pirates demanded to know where in the ship money was hidden but the Dutch refused to tell them. So each member of the crew was dropped overboard one by one in an attempt to loosen Captain Cornelius Williamson's tongue. When he still refused to give in he was half-strangled. Finally the callous robbers took his clothes and threw him into the sea tied to a rope. He was hauled up and cast back eight times before he finally agreed to tell them the information they were after. Taking the valuables the pirates left Williamson, still naked, to bring his crewless ship into port.

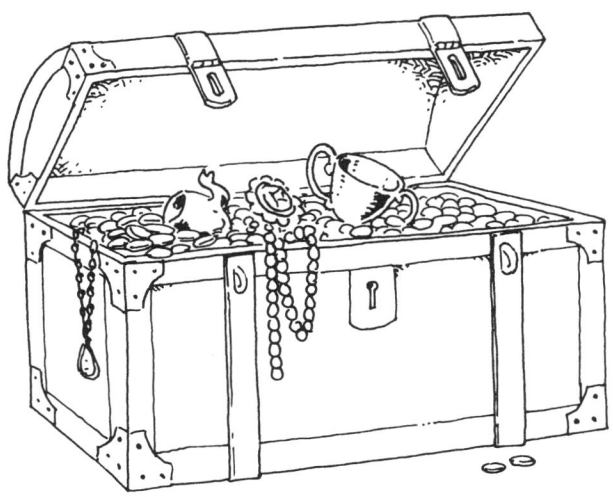

Common myths

Pirates *never* made anyone walk the plank. This idea first surfaced in the minds of Victorian writers to spice up their stories. Perhaps it was inspired by accounts of Roman piracy in which captives thought to be worth little or no ransom were forced overboard and told to swim ashore.

Pirates rarely took a ship's cat aboard. For a start it was associated with too many bad superstitions. And secondly it might eat all the rats, which were considered handy as emergency rations in the event of a food shortage.

Pirate Strongholds

Pirate bases - wherever in the world they were located - quickly became objects of fascination among landlubbers. There would be exotic wines from the Mediterranean, birds of prey from Norway, brightly coloured parrots from Brazil, ivory from Africa, high-quality gold jewellery from the Barbary coast in North Africa and strange coins from far-off lands. People would travel from across the country to see what bargain novelty items could be bought from their hoards. Often the buyers would barter rather than offer cash, and this amazing marketplace would regularly see farmers swapping live cattle for spices, butchers offering bacon for fine clothes or merchants buying wine with a currency of gunpowder and cannon shot.

Considering it was usually illegal, there was little attempt to cover it up. Some of the more confident pirates' crews even allowed local traders to buy on credit - a clear sign that they felt sure of surviving their next sea adventure and would return for settlement of the debt.

The social life was equally bizarre. Pirates with money in their pockets would descend on inns dressed up in the fine clothes of men they had killed. Some even mocked the courts by coming ashore in lawyers' outfits, complete with gowns, powdered wigs and wire spectacles.

Most would get drunk and boast of their bravery to anyone who would listen, all the time keeping an eye out for a girlfriend. Greedier men would gamble with dice, while the more businesslike captains would meet to agree new alliances or sign up additional crew.

Willing novices, wanted men, the unemployed and the starving would all flock to these ports, along with drunken old hands who could get no other skipper to take them on. The inns would serve as recruiting centres, and, of course, they were no place for the ordinary citizens.

A tavern run by a man called Will Mundy on England's south coast was described by one unidentified buccaneer as follows:

'His house is the hell of the world
and he the devil.'

Yet perhaps Mundy needed to present a tough face to the world. Among his regulars was the skipper Stephen Heynes, known for acts of extreme cruelty to those he captured. One story spread like wildfire after Heynes had brought his prize catch - the Danzig-registered ship *Salvator* - into port. It was said that his treatment of the *Salvator* captain was so bad that Heynes's own crew dropped to their knees begging him to stop.

Occasionally, the authorities would try to make an example of pirates. In 1581 the British Admiralty caught a captain called John Piers and hanged him on the cliffs above his home port; the aim was to warn other pirates that their days as unchallenged masters of the coast were over. But when the attacks on shipping showed no signs of stopping, the Navy moved in with a show of strength. Two warships sealed off the anchorage at Studland Bay and commandeered seventeen pirate vessels and three stolen ships. Dozens of skippers were taken in chains to be questioned in the Tower of London and a huge amount of information was gained from them. This included names of their shore accomplices and allowed the authorities to bring a whole string of cases to trial.

But in the end, only nine of the worst offenders were executed. The Queen's advisors realised a war with Spain was likely, and they saw little point in hanging highly experienced seamen who could serve the Navy well. Far from ending their days with a walk to the gallows, most were freed with the Queen's pardon.

Sometimes natural forces - as opposed to military ones - were responsible for wiping out pirate bases. Port Royal, in Jamaica, was a hotbed of activity for much of the 17th century. But in 1692 a powerful earthquake hit the town, the ground opened up and a massive tidal wave crashed in. Whole streets disappeared ... along with most of the resident scoundrels.

Easily defended island strongholds were a firm favourite among pirate captains, especially if their governments had given them permission to attack enemy shipping. The island of Lundy, for instance, in England's Bristol Channel, became a fortress for French and Spanish pirates during centuries of naval warfare with the English.

In the 1660s a French crew plotted to take over the island by posing as Dutchmen (at the time the Netherlands was seen as a reliable ally in the struggle with France). The pirates claimed they needed milk for their sick captain and the trusting islanders provided it for five days. Then the visitors said their skipper had died and asked

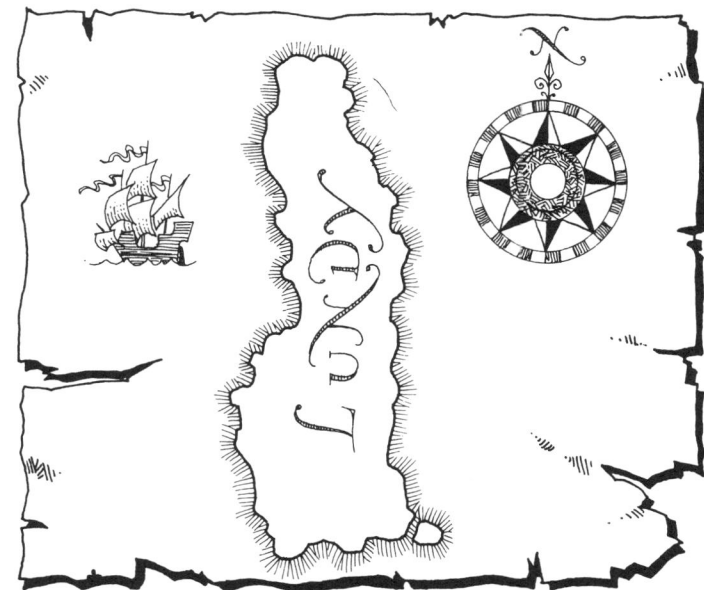

the islanders to wait outside. They then lifted off the coffin lid, grabbed the guns hidden inside and imprisoned the entire population. They escaped with all the valuables they could find and as many farm animals as they could fit into the ship's hold.

Lundy later became home to bands of Turks and Africans who recognised the rich pickings to be had from merchant vessels sailing home from the New World.

THE PIRATE SHIP

PLEASE NOTE THAT LEFT AND RIGHT ARE AS VIEWED FROM THE STERN OF THE SHIP.

You will need an ordinary craft knife with renewable blades, a small pair of scissors and an ordinary ball-point pen that has run out of ink.

Use a small tube of contact adhesive glue, the sort that goes onto each surface to be stuck and is then left to dry for a few moments before the parts are pressed together. You will also need a small amount of white PVA glue, carpenters' water-soluble glue which dries clear. This is used for 'spot gluing' and laminating flags and banners together, etc.

Work in a well-lit area where you can leave your model parts without them being damaged. Use a plastic cutting board or a thick sheet of cardboard to protect furniture.

Remove model pages from the book before cutting them to shape. Read the instructions and look at the drawings to ensure you understand the assembly stages before starting to cut the parts. If you are not sure, go back over the instructions.

Only cut the parts as you need them in assembly. Cut along the solid black lines, press just enough to cut through the card and cut slowly.

Crease the dotted lines with the ball-point pen, run it along gently to make a mark and then go over to make a deeper crease. Try this on a piece of scrap card first to see how it works.

Do not apply glue straight from the tube. Use a strip of thick card like a narrow brush to spread the glue exactly where it is needed on the hatched glue areas. Use these areas to position the parts.

Line up the parts before pressing them into place. Take your time, don't rush, and check every step first.

As soon as the hull is complete you can sit it on the stand to make the next stages easier to do.

STEP 1

Curve Bow to shape and glue at A.
Fold down top decking and glue flaps to outer surface of Bow at B. Note that three flaps are cut out at C.

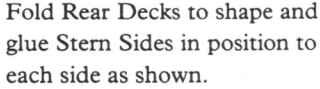

STEP 2

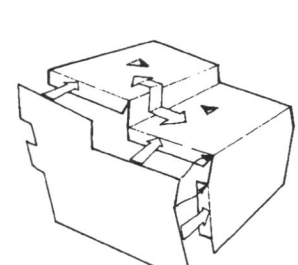

Fold Rear Decks to shape and glue Stern Sides in position to each side as shown.

Fold Stern to shape to form stepped shape. Glue longest glue flap at top first to Rear Deck, followed by shorter flaps at A.

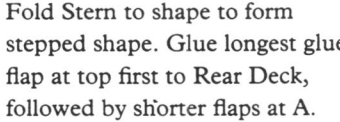

Curve Stern Sides and glue in position, lining up at lower edge B.

STEP 3

Form Rear Cabin Window to shape and glue flaps at A and B.
Shape rounded flaps as shown.

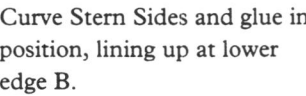

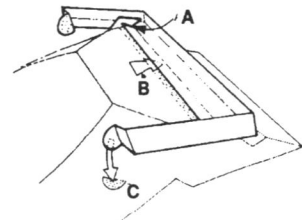

Slide Cabin Windows over stern and locate over tab each side at A. Glue long flap into position at B. Fold down sides and glue flaps at C.

STEP 4

Fold Middle Deck to shape with mast cutout A towards stern. Stand Bow and Stern on flat surface and see how Middle Deck lines up between them. Glue Middle Deck to outside of Bow and Stern at B. Glue long flaps C.
Ensure you know how parts line up before assembly.

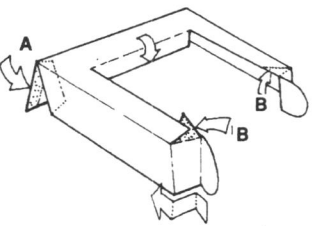

STEP 5

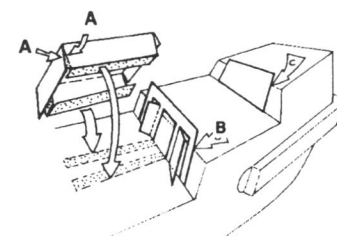

Fold Deck Cabin to shape and glue end at A. Glue onto Deck to marks arrowed.
Glue Middle Wall at B and Back Wall at C.

STEP 6

Shape Fore Deck and glue to tabs at A and glue flap at B.
Glue Front Wall in position at C.

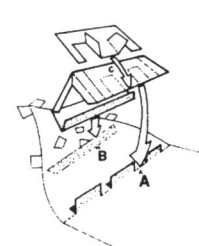

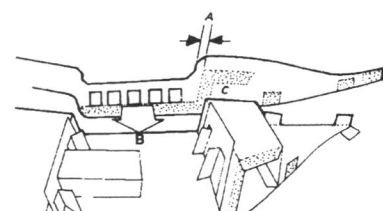

STEP 7

Position Side Rails as shown, line up lower edges of Gun Ports with edge of Deck at B and position upper edge 3 mm forward of Fore Deck as indicated at A. Glue in position as per shaded areas. Glue two small flaps to Prow.

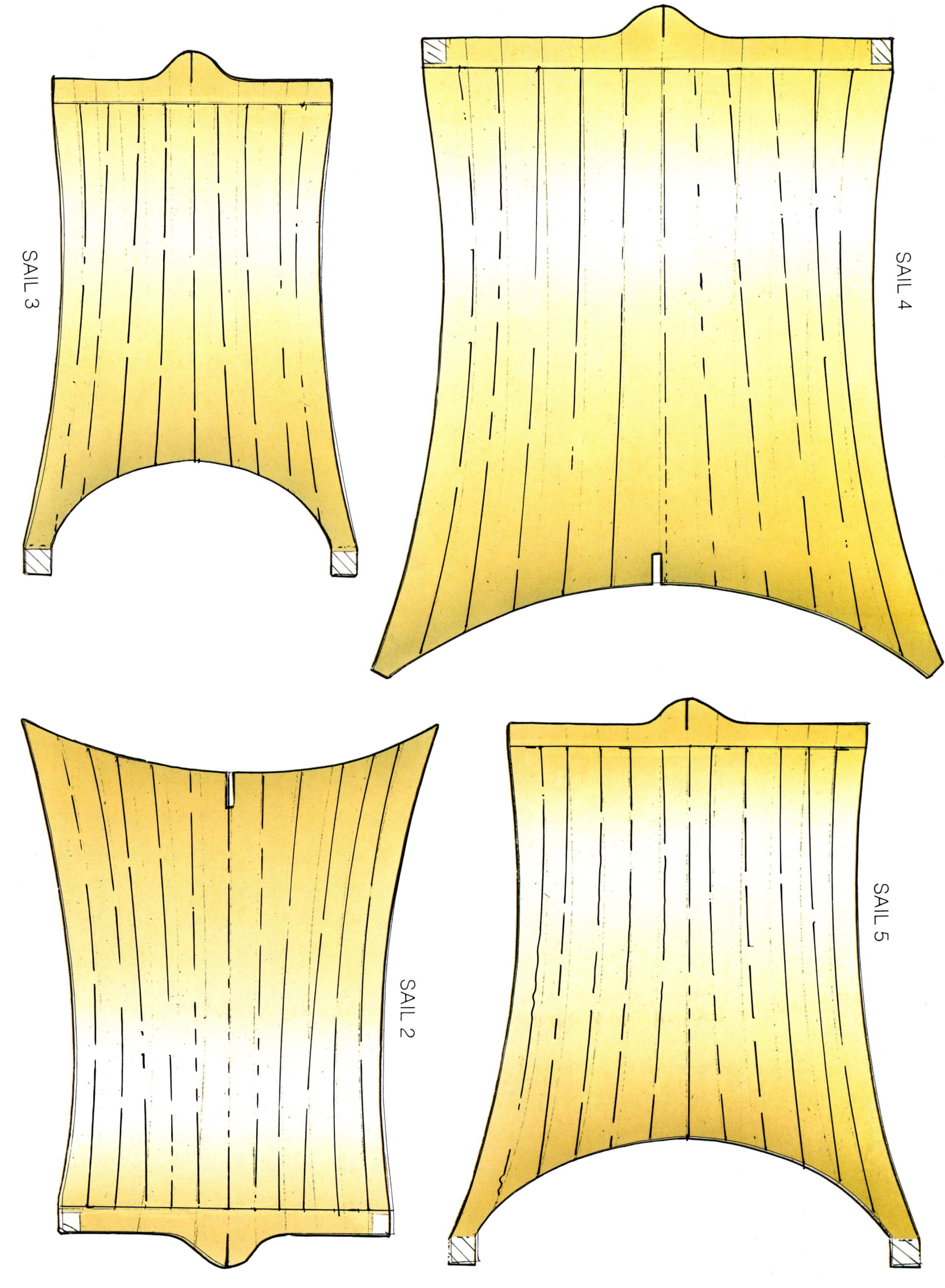

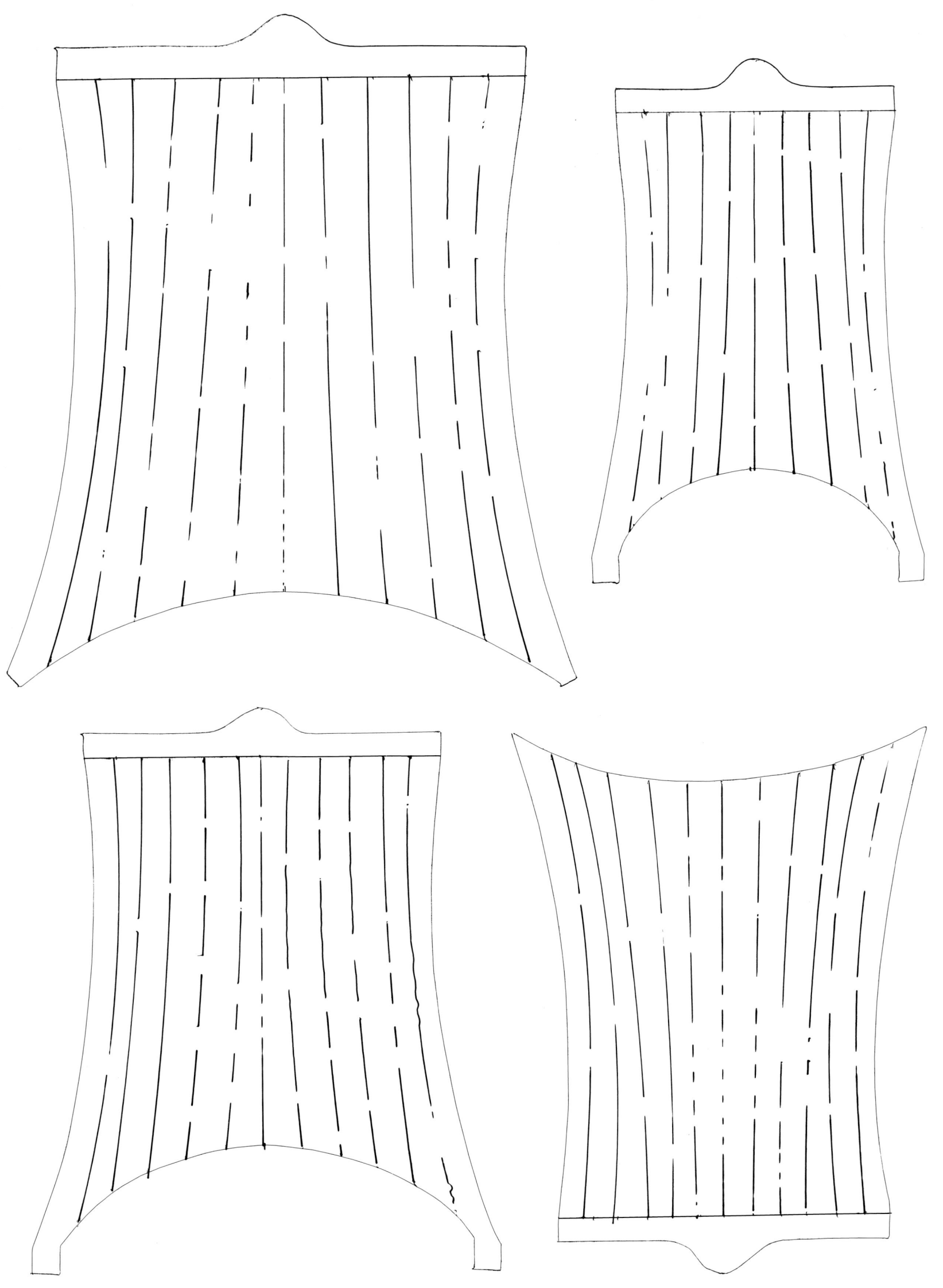

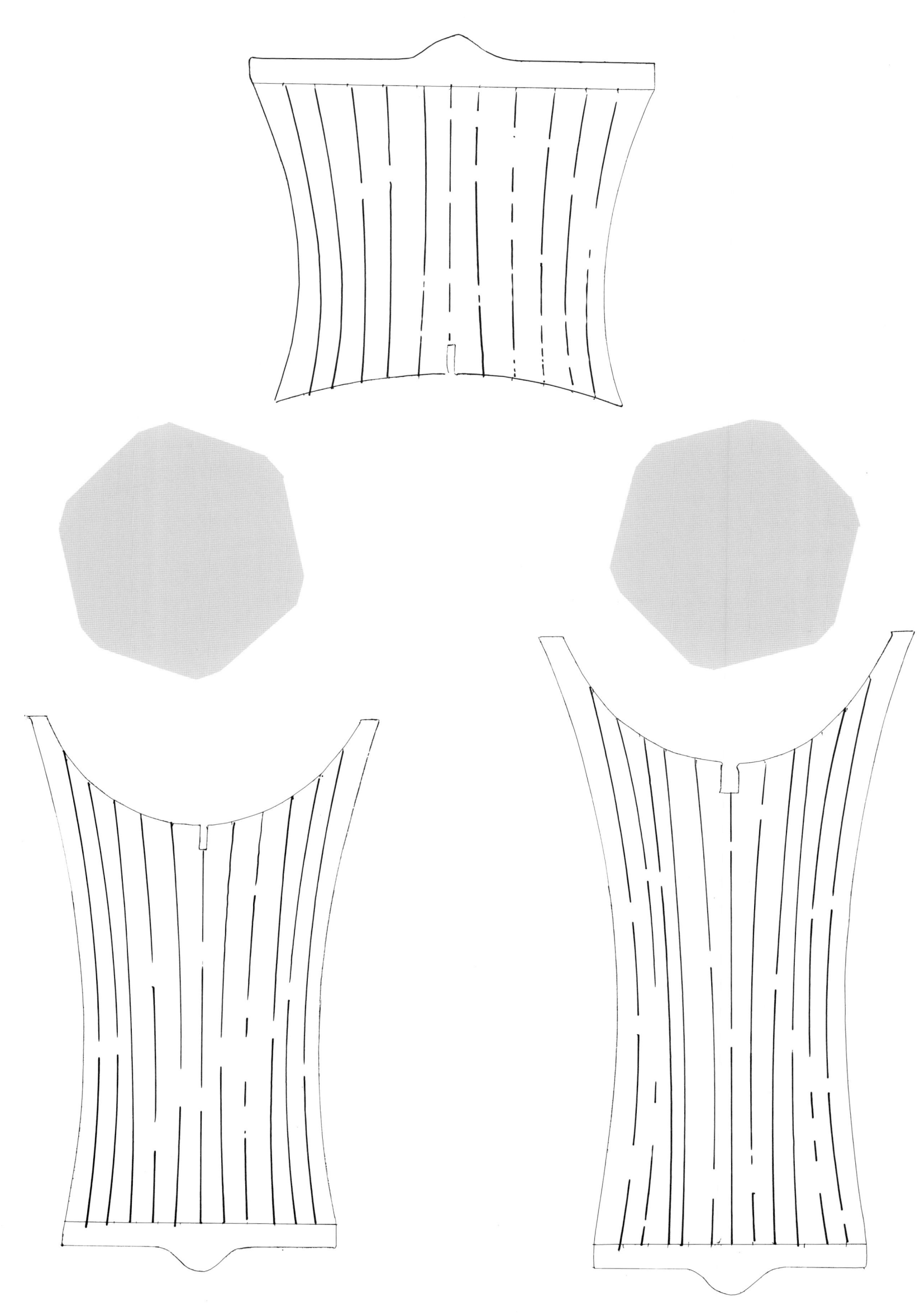

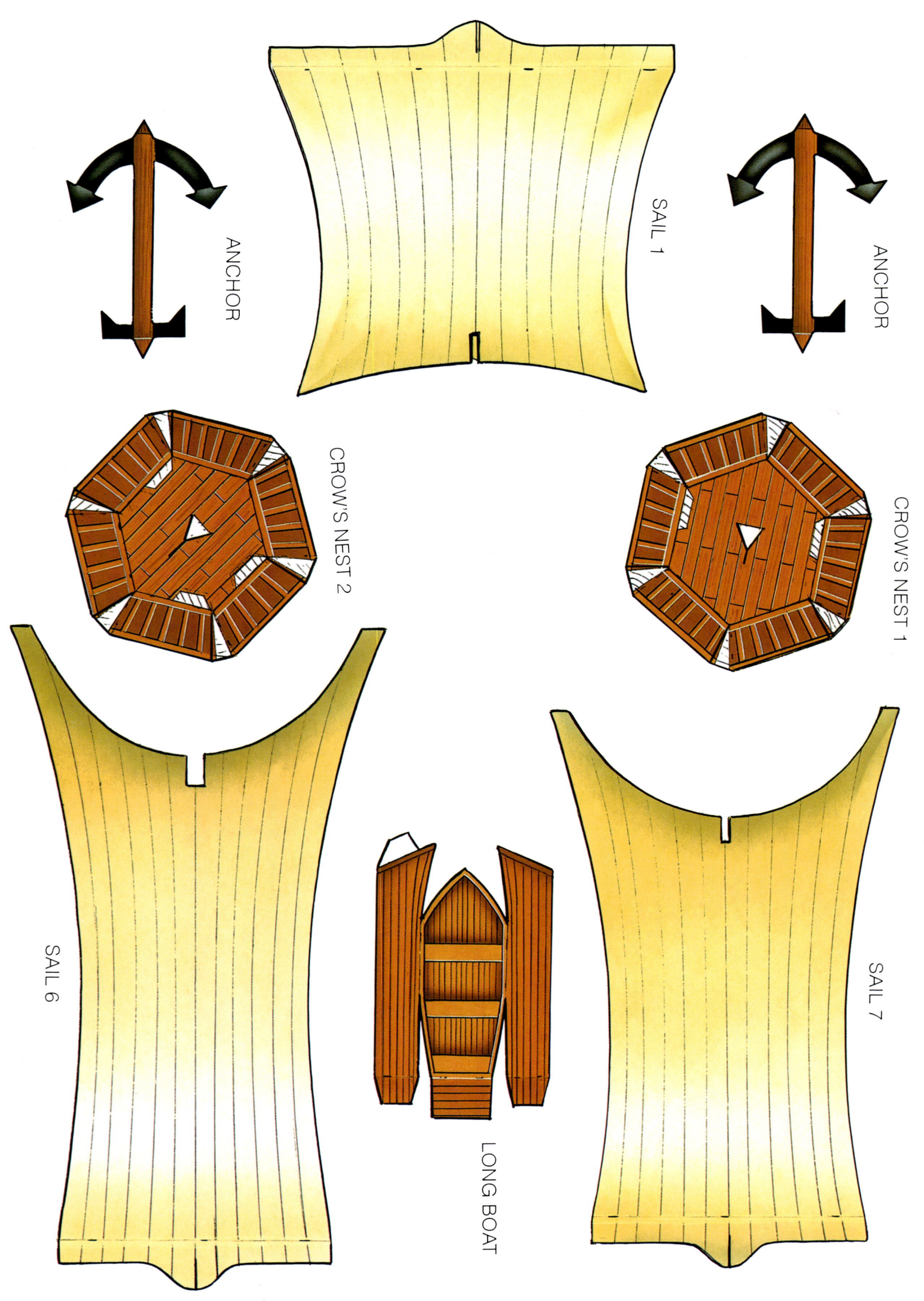

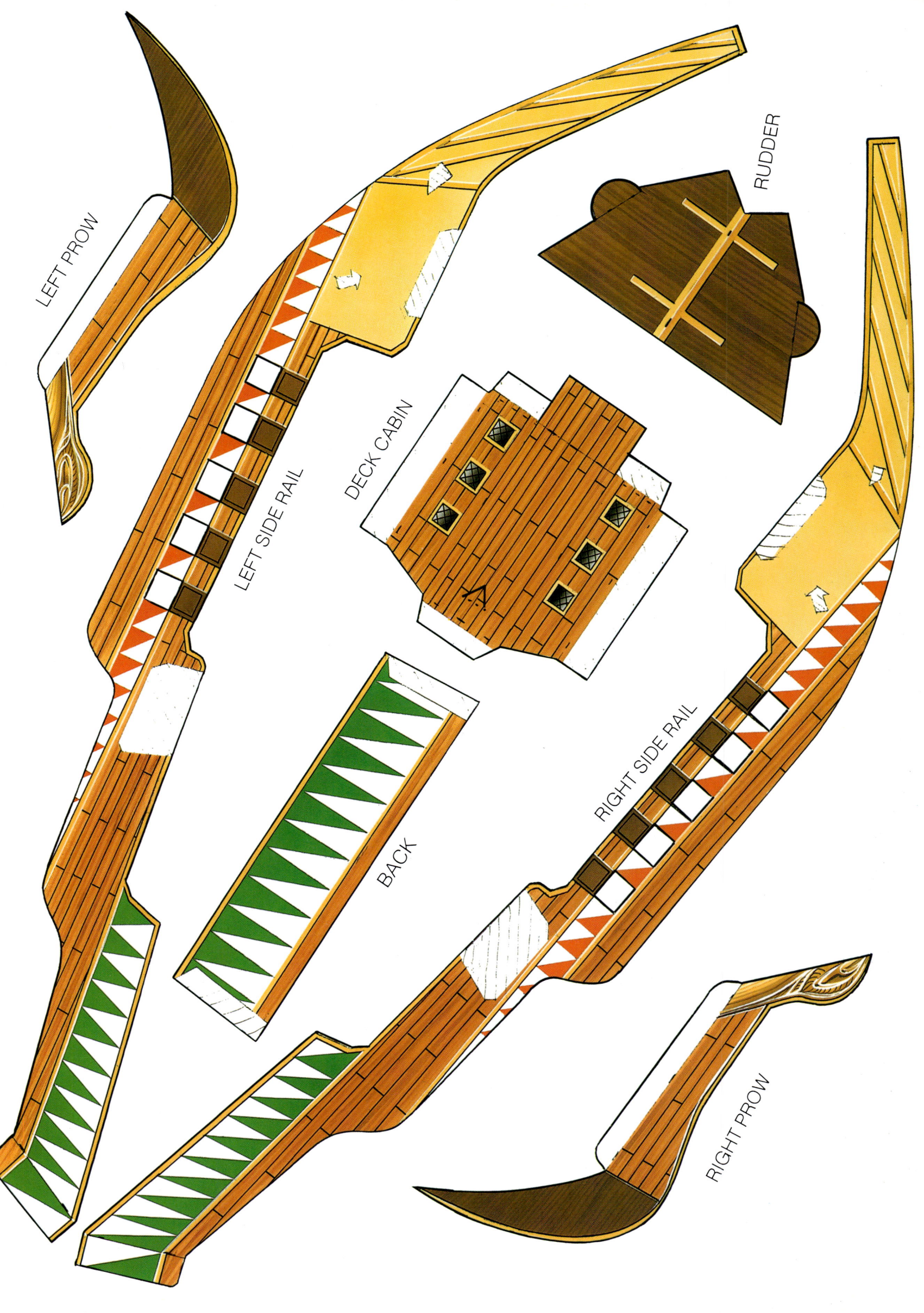

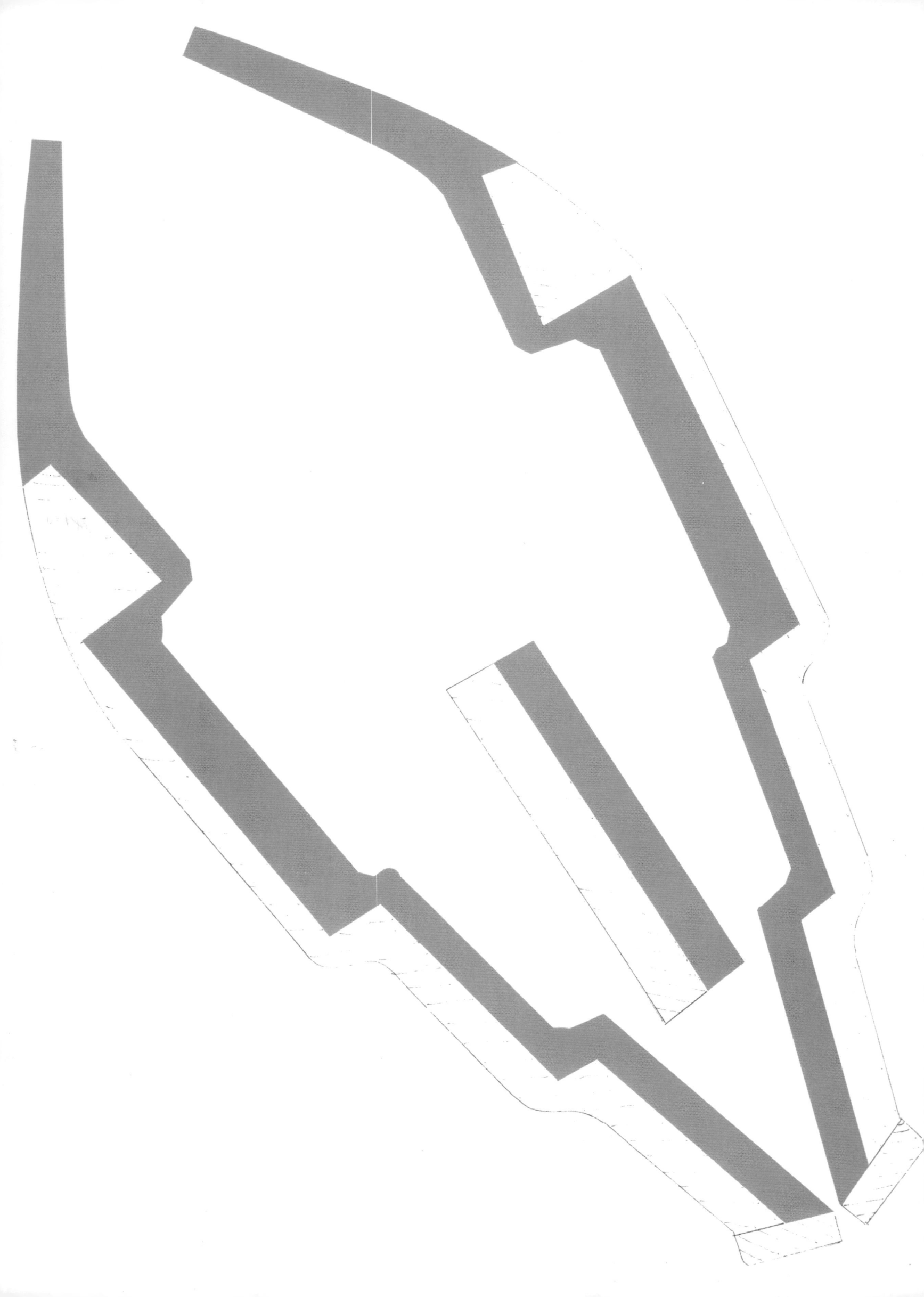

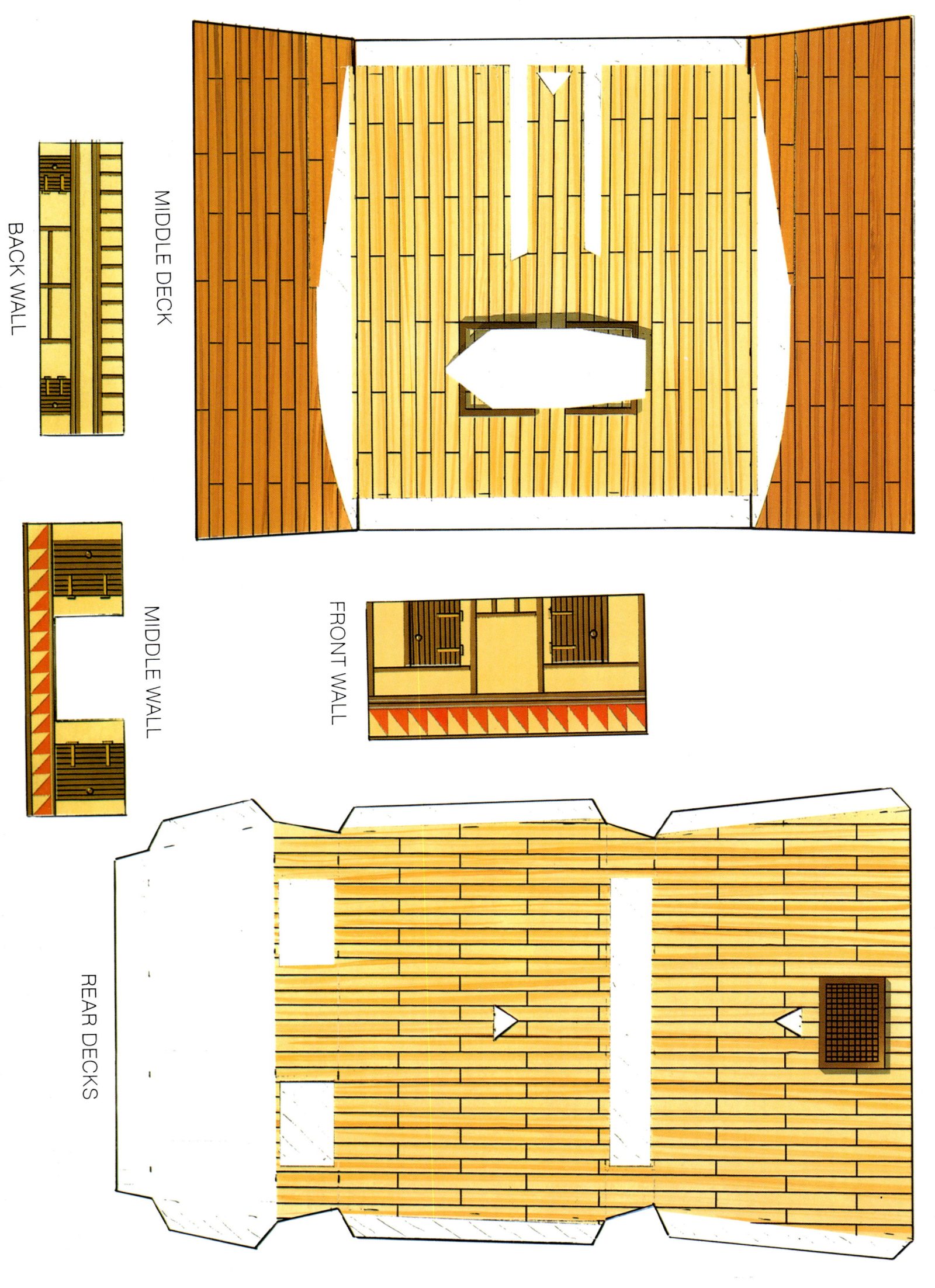

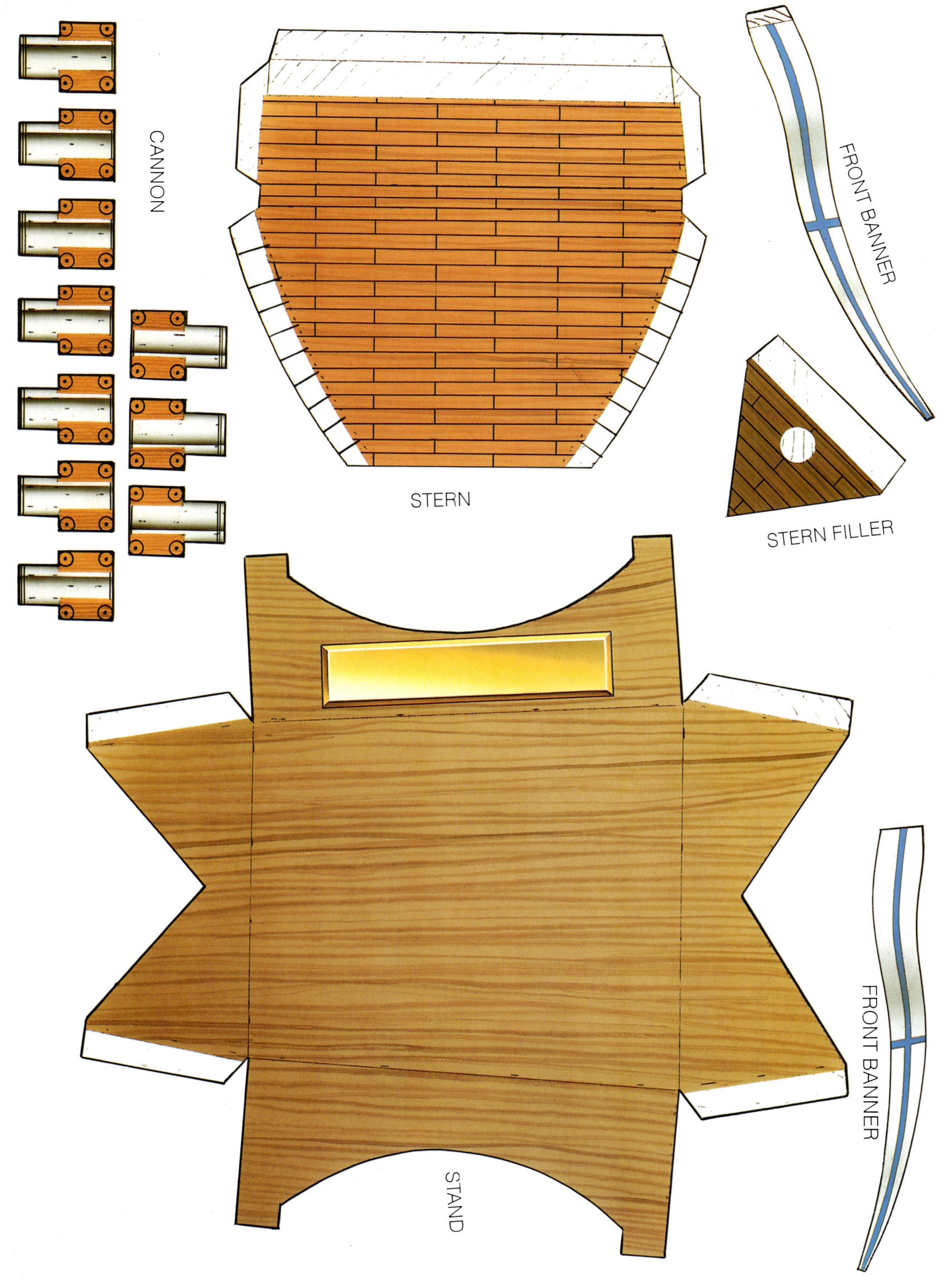

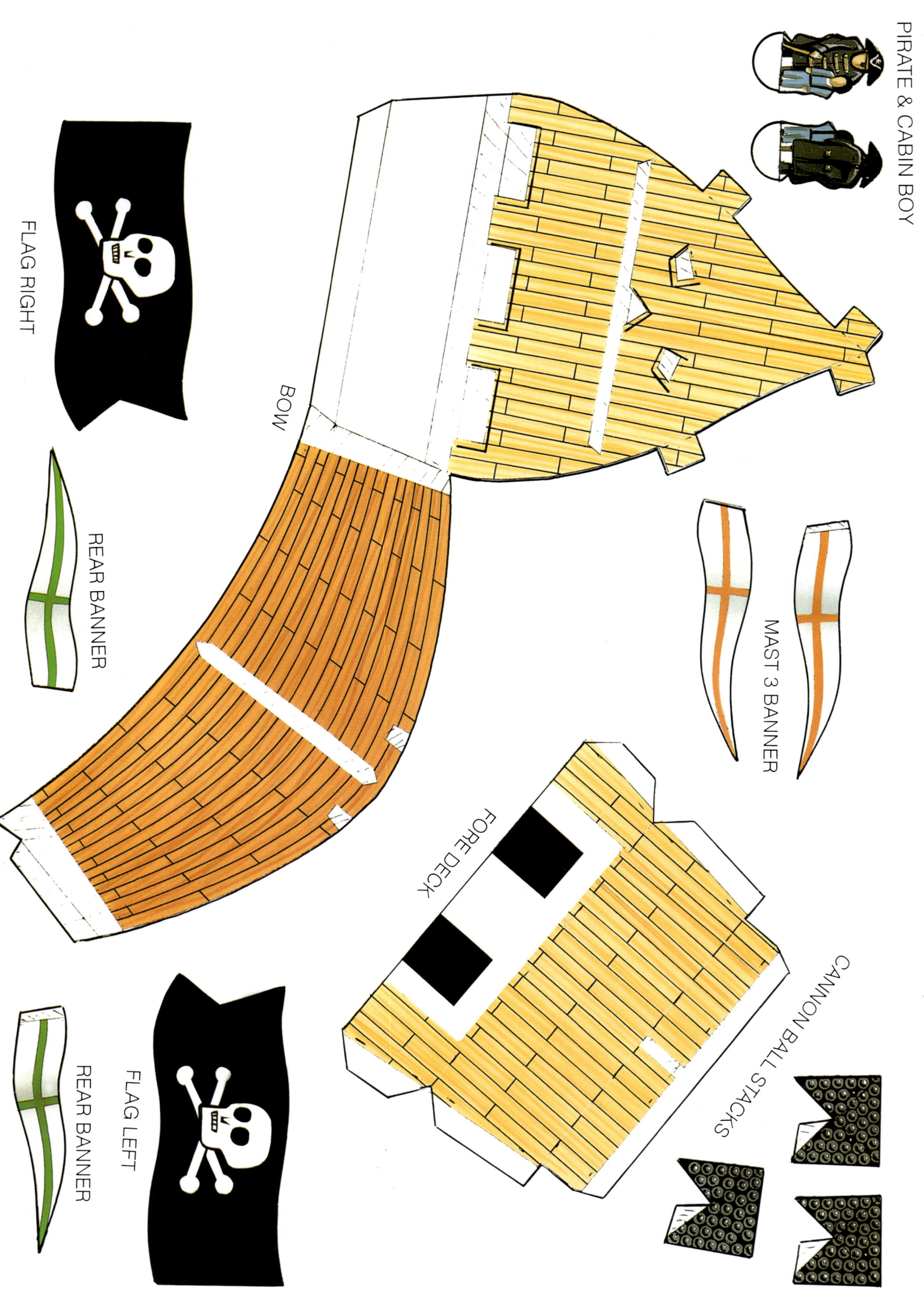

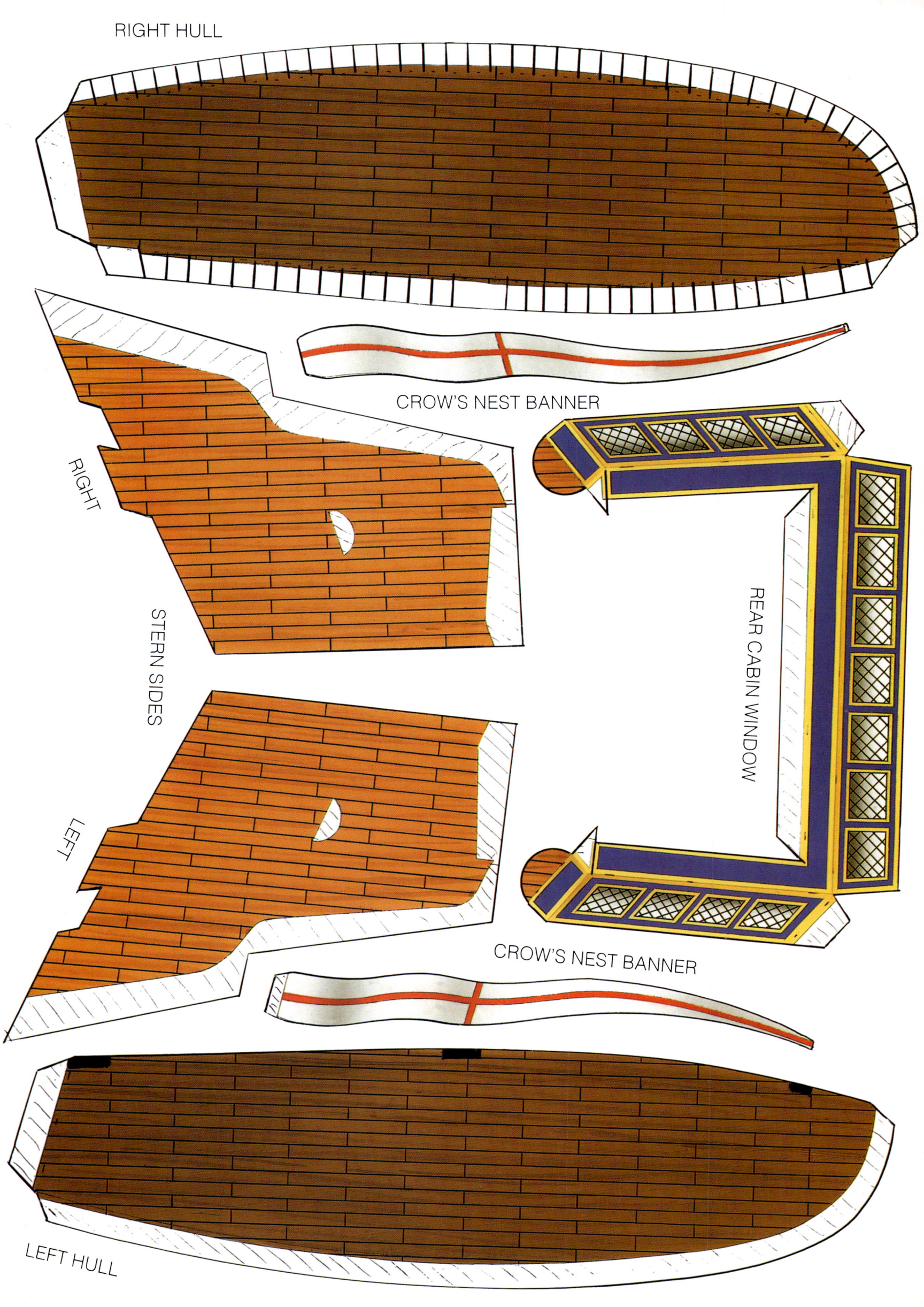

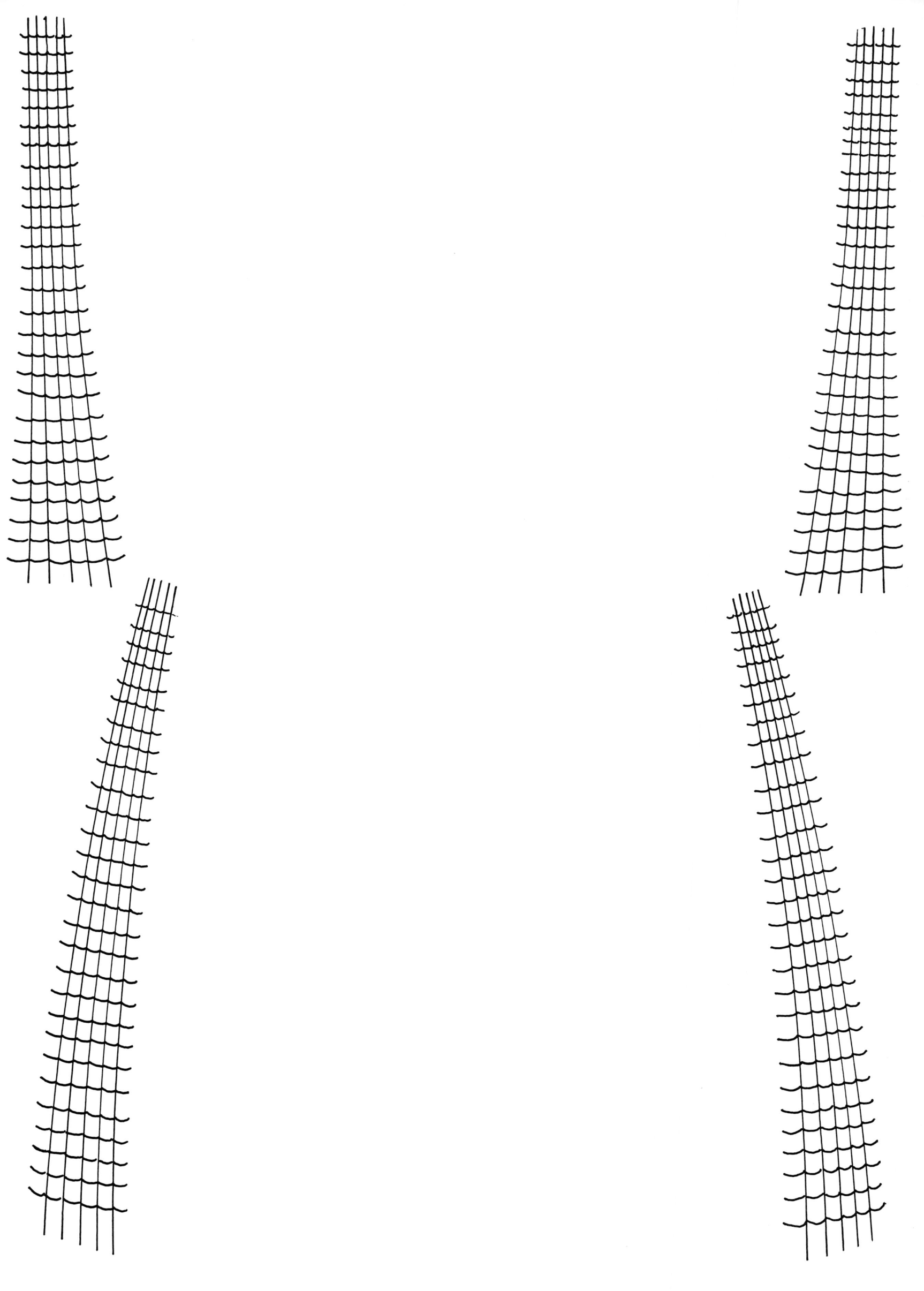

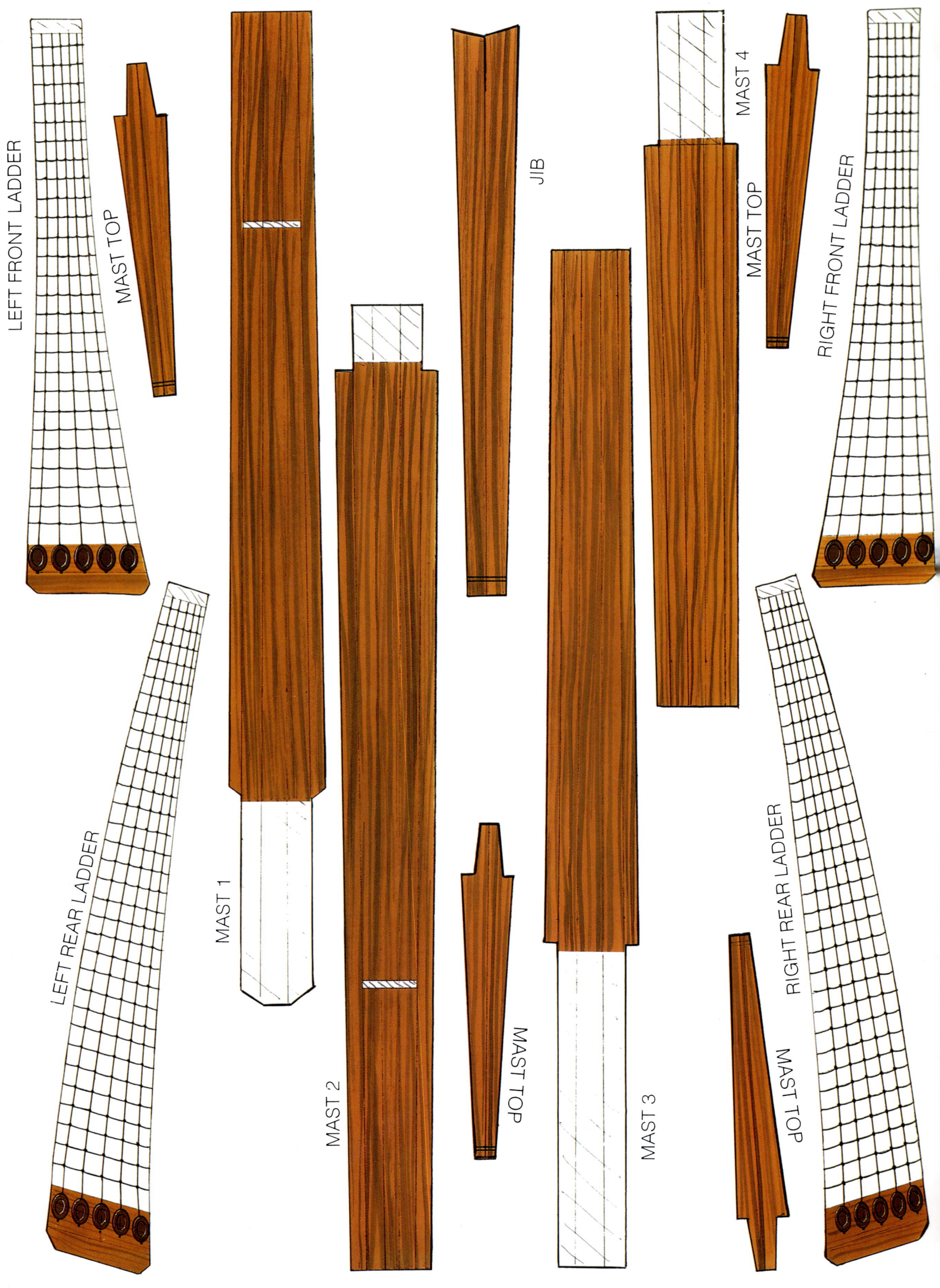

STEP 8

Hold Side Rail against side of ship and position back strip to line up with top edge at A. Glue back strip in position.
Bend Side Rail out and apply glue to top edge of decks and glue Side Rail in position. Finally, glue end flap at B.

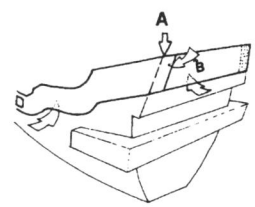

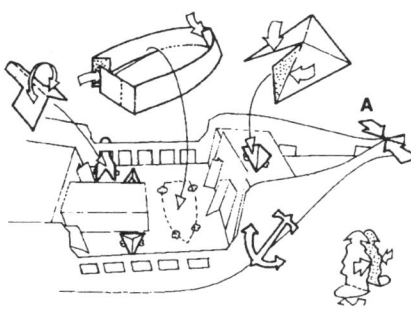

STEP 9

Glue tip of Side Rail at A.
Glue the Pirate halves back to back. Bend up flaps.
Fold the Cannon Ball stacks and glue to shape. Spot glue in positions shown.
Fold Long Boat to shape, glue front and rear tabs and spot glue to position marked on deck.
Fold Cannons to shape and spot glue to deck with barrel through Gun Port.
Glue Anchors to each Side Rail in position as marked.

STEP 10

Carefully curve Hull halves as arrowed. See how the two parts join centrally. Again, curve the completed shape and see how it fits into the Hull opening. Apply glue to inner edge of Hull and flaps of Hull halves. Start at front centre as marked and carefully work along each edge left and right, pressing the join together, until the rear opening is formed.

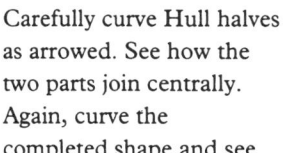
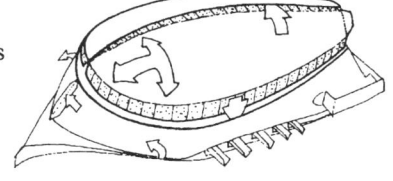

STEP 11

Fold Rudder and glue flat as shown.
Glue the Prow halves together as arrowed at A. Glue front edges together as arrowed.

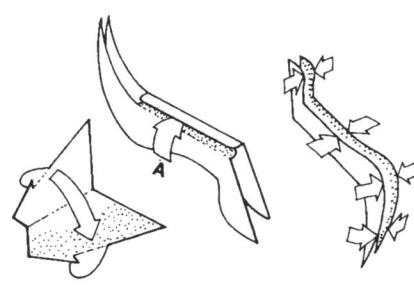

STEP 12

Fold and glue the Stand to shape. Note that the wider end fits the Bow of the ship.

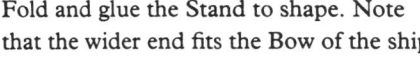

STEP 13

Glue the Stern Filler onto the hull. Glue the Rudder in position.

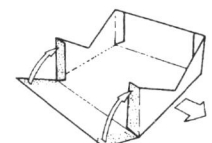
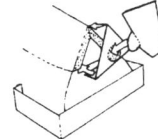

STEP 14

Glue the Prow to the centre mark on Bow at A and spot glue at each end arrrowed.

STEP 15

Fold to shape and glue the corners of the two Crow's Nests 1 and 2.

Fold and glue Jib.
Do not glue curved-out end strips.
Fold Masts from 1 to 4 to shape and glue edges together as arrowed.
Fold and glue Mast Tops and glue each one into the top of a Mast; note how shaped join matches up.
Check the Masts as they dry and ensure they are straight.

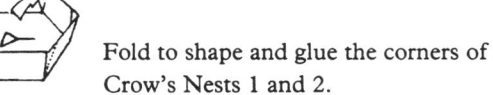

STEP 16

Glue the halves of the four Banners together back to back as shown at A. Do the same to the Flag at B. Curve them all to shape as they dry.
Slide Crow's Nest 1 onto Mast 1 and spot glue to the white line on the Mast. Do the same to Mast 2.
Glue the Banners to the Masts as indicated. Glue the Crow's Nest Banner to the underside of Crow's Nest 2.
The Masts slide through the triangular holes and cuts. Apply plenty of glue to the end of the Mast to be glued and to the stepped joint that locates it in the hole. Feed the Mast through the hole and feel how it touches the Hull inside. Ensure the Mast is properly upright and leave to dry.
Glue the Jib to the base of Mast 1 and spot glue it as arrowed at C. Leave everything to dry thoroughly. Place ship on Stand.

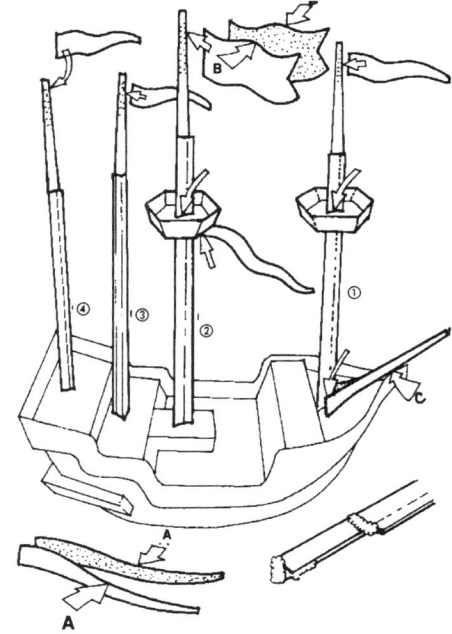

STEP 17

Ladders are indicated Front and Rear. Fold over tabs at top and glue them to the underside of the Crow's Nests and the lower ends to the positions as marked on the Side Rails.

STEP 18

All Sails are curved and spot glued to the Masts and Jib.

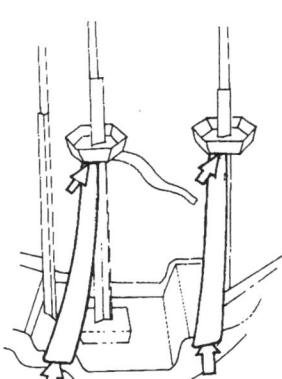
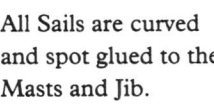
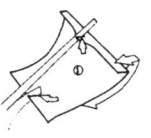

Apply a spot of glue to the slits at top and bottom of each Sail, fold the top edge and push the Sail over the Jib as arrowed.

STEP 19

Mast 1.
Glue Sail in position at 1 as shown.
Glue top of Sail 3 to Mast and glue small flaps to top edge of Sail 2 as shown.
Repeat for Mast 2.

STEP 20

Glue Sail 6 in position as before to Mast 3.
Repeat for Mast 4.

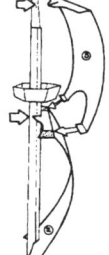
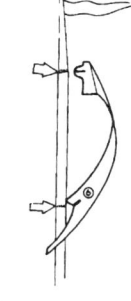

Choose a name for your ship and write it in the box on the stand.

THE WORLD'S BEST-KNOWN PIRATES

BLACKBEARD

Otherwise known as Edward Teach, Blackbeard was among the most bloodthirsty skippers ever to step onto a ship, and looked every inch as deadly as his reputation. He got his nickname by braiding his long, black beard and tying up the ends with ribbons. Though it might seem ridiculous by today's standards, Blackbeard believed it made him attractive. It seems he could not get enough girlfriends and is said to have had 14 different wives in his life.

Blackbeard's hunting ground was along the American coast of Virginia and North Carolina. Many on land believed he operated under the protection of the North Carolina governor, although nothing was ever proved. During the early 18th century he terrorised the local merchants in his vessel, *The Queen Anne's Revenge,* by lurking in rivers or behind sand banks to ambush them. He would also try to trick his opponents into believing he was some kind of earth-devil by sticking long, flaming matches under his hat. These would light up his face, making him look like some supernatural spirit. If that didn't have the right effect he would toss the matches into pots of sulphur to cause mini explosions.

Blackbeard was a great believer that rum solved many of life's problems, and he drank enormous quantities. Guests taking dinner in his gloomy cabin would be terrified when, after a few glasses of drink, he would pull out one of his pistols and start shooting underneath the table.

Blackbeard also believed a sober crew was a dangerous crew. In his diary, he claimed the men would act like a confused rabble and plot against him if they had no strong drink, but as long as they were supplied with good rum everything on the ship ran smoothly!

Eventually the Virginia planters and growers, whose trade had suffered badly at the hands of Blackbeard, pressed for action against him. Confronted by an angry mob, the state governor sent out HMS *Pearl* to take the pirate dead or alive.

Blackbeard was caught on 21 November 1718, near Ocracoke Inlet off the North Carolina coast. Typically, he died fighting - his sword and a pistol in his hand to the last. Doctors later found he had 25 severe wounds and probably succumbed to loss of blood. His head was brought back to Virginia in triumph and stuck up on a pole for all to see.

WILLIAM KIDD

Kidd began his career raiding French ships. But in 1695 the British king William III commissioned him as a privateer with the task of rounding up a particularly bothersome bunch of pirates. Kidd left New York in September 1696 and headed across the Atlantic to Africa. He captured two French-flagged ships (Britain and France were at war so this was considered a legal act) but fought no pirate ships. Later, he headed for Madagascar and became firm friends with the very pirates he'd been sent to kill.

Many of Kidd's crew deserted him on the East African coast, but Kidd still had enough men to get him back to the West Indies. There he discovered he had been officially declared a pirate and decided to set up a nest-egg in America, in case he was ever forced to go into hiding. He left gold, silver and Indian artefacts with friends in New York. He was arrested as he walked down the gangplank in Boston.

Back in England, Kidd was then told he was accused of five acts of piracy and the murder of a gunner, William Moore. He was denied legal advice, found guilty and hanged. Many stories and legends have since been based on Captain Kidd's priceless treasure. The most famous of all is *Treasure Island*, by Robert Louis Stevenson.

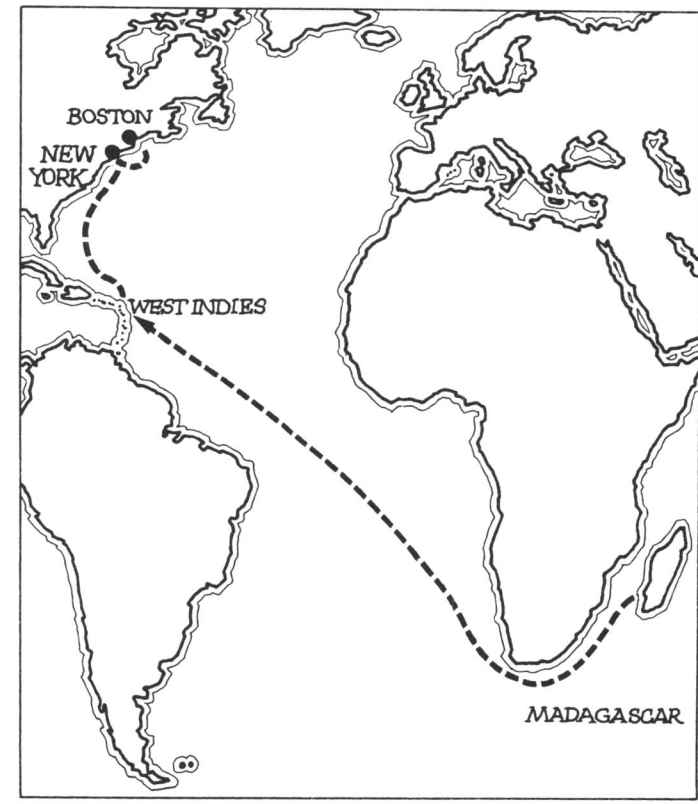

SIR HENRY MORGAN

Captain Morgan, among the best known of the international buccaneers, first turned up in the West Indies in 1655. He was then a humble soldier serving with a raiding party which managed to capture the Spanish colony of Jamaica.

Morgan based himself on the island and by the 1660s he was busy raiding and harassing Spanish ships. The new governor of Jamaica, Thomas Modyford, thought buccaneers were the best defence against Spain's domination, and he gave Morgan his blessing. The captain threw himself into his work with delight and, in 1668, pulled off his first big success. He led a force of around 500 buccaneers against Portobello, Panama, and took over the city. His tactics were at times ruthless. At one point, he ordered his men to use priests and prisoners as a human shield during their assault on a fortress.

The following year, Morgan led his 'private army' in a fleet of eight ships against the city of Maracaibo, Venezuela. On his way back he was surprised by three large Spanish warships. They had orders to hunt him down and kill him because he was such a threat. But Morgan's force was far too strong and he easily fought them off. When he finally docked in Jamaica it was to hear news that England and Spain were close to a peace treaty. The governor was worried about letting Morgan loose again because he realised it could upset the talks. However, he at last agreed, and Morgan left before the news that peace had been declared came through.

In December 1670, he led his largest and most famous attack on Panama. Morgan had assembled 38 ships, carrying more than 2,000 seamen, in an attempt to gain control of the country. He captured several towns before marching on Panama City in 1671.

The Spaniards resorted to desperate measures and tried to see Morgan off by stampeding a herd of cattle at his men. They also started fires in outer parts of the city to slow down his advance. Neither tactic worked. The cattle were scattered and the Spanish army behind them

slaughtered. As for the fires - they got totally out of control and destroyed most of the city.

When Morgan got back to Jamaica he found his old friend Modyford had been sacked and replaced by a new governor. Morgan was arrested and sent to England for trial. But Charles II intervened and not only forgave the buccaneer but knighted him as well. Morgan was installed as lieutenant governor of Jamaica and stayed on the island until his death in 1688.

THE BARBAROSSA BROTHERS

They ruled the seas in the Mediterranean during the early 1500s, and consequently made a fortune. They attacked Christian ships from their bases on the North African and Turkish coasts and were well supported by their fellow Muslims. The name *Barbarossa* (it means red beard) was given them because both men sported bushy ginger beards beneath their turbans. Arouj Barbarossa was killed in battle but his brother Khery-ed-Din went on to enjoy his huge wealth and become a national hero in Turkey.

BARTHOLOMEW 'BLACK BART' ROBERTS

He was reckoned to have captured and robbed well over 400 ships during the early 18th century. He would roam the whole of the Atlantic, from the Caribbean to East Africa.

JOHN AVERY

His ship, the *Fancy,* scoured the Red Sea looking for merchant ships during the late 17th century. His greatest prizes tended to be treasure-packed vessels coming from India, which belonged to the Great Mogul. Despite amassing great wealth he eventually returned to England and lost it all in a bad business decision. He died poor and with few friends.

ANNE BONNEY AND MARY READ

They were among the very few women pirates of the 18th century and both served aboard the same ship. Anne fell in love with the renowned pirate Calico Jack Rackham after joining his crew.

THE PRIVATEERS

PERHAPS THE THREE MOST FAMOUS privateers were all Englishmen and all knights of the realm. Sir Francis Drake, Sir Walter Raleigh and Sir John Hawkins were the 'official' pirates of Queen Elizabeth I and each fought the Spanish with great fervour, to the delight of Her Majesty.

The English quarrel with Spain centred on the fact that Spain's explorers had found the New World first and claimed it for their king. England was effectively shut out of the trade that sprung up, and therefore resolved that what she could not take by agreement, she would steal.

20TH-CENTURY PIRATES

THE PIRATES OF TODAY BEAR LITTLE resemblance to those who brought terror to the waves in the days of Blackbeard and the Barbarossa brothers. Today's pirate uses small, fast powerboats, arms him/herself to the teeth, with automatic weapons and prefers to attack under cover of night.

But two things have not changed. First, the lust for wealth. And second, the bloodthirsty nature of the attacks.

The Philippines, South China Sea, Indian Ocean, West Africa, the Caribbean and South America are among the most feared areas for pirate raids. In the early 1980s, up to 12 merchant ships a day were reporting attacks by raiders in the West Africa area alone. Other victims of recent years have been Vietnamese boat people - refugees who have fled their country with their last remaining possessions.

No one doubts that piracy is on the increase. It has certainly become easier as the size of crews has become smaller (the result of ship owners trying to save money). There is also less risk of the pirates finding themselves caught by a naval warship or gunboat. Most of the world's navies are much smaller than they once were, and poorer countries simply cannot afford the extra costs of patrolling these dangerous waters. Very often, a few unarmed merchant seamen are left to fight teams of professional pirates who easily outnumber them.

In the South China Sea, especially, piracy remains a way of life. Children are brought up hearing stories of the days, in the 19th century, when a woman commanded a fleet of almost 800 pirate junks and 70,000 men. The gang was eventually wiped out by naval forces but over the years new, and ever more cruel, pirates have emerged to take their place.

Some countries, however, have made it clear they will not allow their ships to be robbed so easily. The former Soviet Union armed all merchant ships bound for dangerous waters. Although the Soviets never boasted about how they dealt with pirate attacks their attitude was clear. In one case, a Soviet vessel arrived in Singapore harbour towing a small, empty craft behind it. The captain said he had found it abandoned and nobody could prove otherwise, but everyone guessed the truth. The small boat had belonged to pirates who attacked what they thought would be an easy target. The Soviet gunmen treated them without mercy.

Not only big merchant ships are at risk. Pirates also prey on small yachts, reckoning the sailors aboard them will have plenty of valuables that can be resold at the nearest market. Experts advise yachtsmen sailing near known pirate nests to arm themselves and fire before the attackers get in too close. Pleasure cruisers are warned to stay within the busier sea lanes so that they stand some chance of getting help in the event of attack. Sailors who set off in search of some remote palm-fringed deserted island are asking for trouble.

 # Hidden Treasure

Amateur divers and treasure hunters dream of making their fortune by finding a pirate hoard. Below are a few of the most popular locations to hunt.

Ocracoke Inlet, North Carolina: Blackbeard was said to have stashed huge amounts of gold and silver bullion here. Every year hundreds of treasure hunters try to find the lost hoard - so far without success.

Cocos Island, near Costa Rica: The island is thought to have the 'Lost Loot of Lima' hidden in its ground. The treasure is believed to be worth a staggering £40 million and was buried by Benito Bonito, captain of the *Bloody Sword*.

Oak Island, Nova Scotia: Here, treasure hunters regularly try to reach the bottom of a deep shaft which, it is said, connects to a labyrinth of underground tunnels in which pirate bounty is stored. No one has got in yet, because the shaft keeps filling up with sea water.

Somewhere in the Pacific Ocean, off the coast of South America, lies one of the best-hidden hoards of all time. Hundreds of pieces of silver were captured by a particularly dim pirate band who decided their booty was in fact tin. They tossed the whole lot overboard. In today's currency it would have been worth millions.

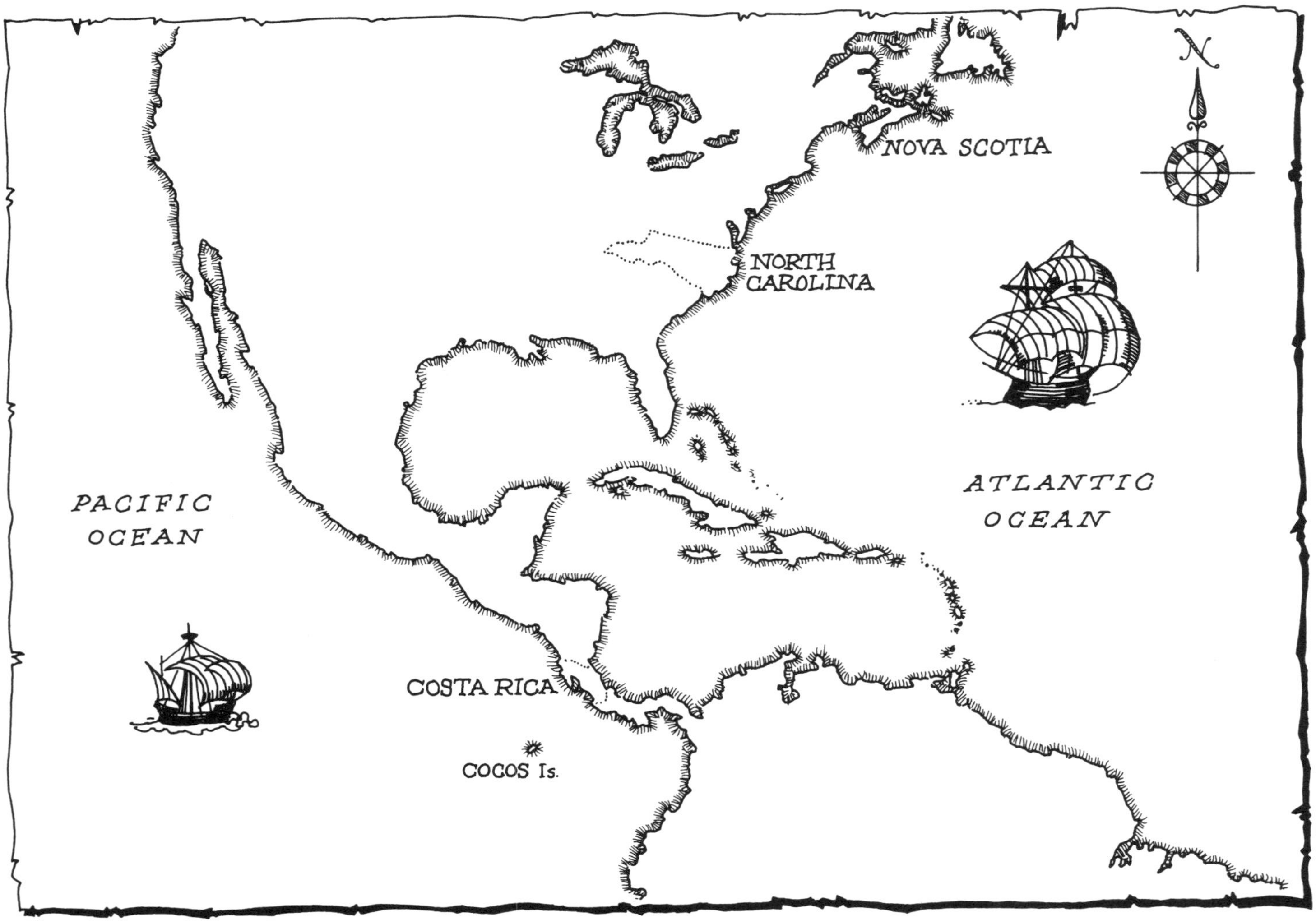